Colchester. Since that time the size and quality of the archaeology collections have continued to develop, particularly through the extensive excavations within the town by the Colchester Archaeological Trust.

The collections are not just restricted to Colchester or the Roman period as, in the early years, material was acquired from other parts of Essex. In particular, from 1855 an arrangement was entered into which enabled the collections of the Essex Archaeological Society to be housed with those of Colchester Borough Council. In 1926 the two collections were formally amalgamated, with the Council taking on full management of the museum.

excavated outer works, was opened in 1935.

The status of the collections was further enhanced in the 1930s with the important excavations at the late Iron Age and early Roman site at Sheepen, on the north-west edge of

ABOVE **Egyptian mummy-case of Lady Tahathor from the end of the 26th Dynasty, about 550 BC. The mummy was bought in Egypt for £7 by George Errington of Lexden Park in 1856 and given to the museum in 1871.**

ABOVE **Visit of Queen Mary to the recently reopened museum in June 1938.**

LEFT **A London and North Eastern Railway poster by Fred Taylor, dating from 1931, advertising Colchester as a place to visit.**

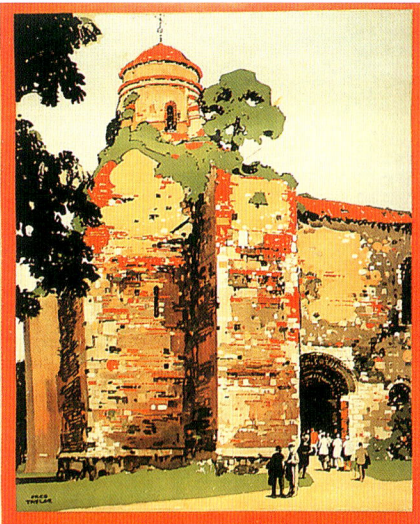

COLCHESTER

EXPRESS SERVICES AND CHEAP FARES
BY L·N·E·R

Illustrated Guide Free from Town Clerk, Town Hall Colchester

What is Archaeology?

It is nearly impossible to find anywhere in our crowded landscape where our ancestors have not been before.

Archaeology is the study of the traces – in all their forms – that have been left by our ancestors. It is often like detective work, gathering together information and uncovering the evidence hidden for generations. This is not simply a fanciful comparison, as is shown by the increasing interest of the police in the techniques used by archaeologists to excavate and recover information from buried remains.

Archaeologists recover evidence in layers. These layers are created by natural means, human activity or a combination of both. When archaeologists excavate a site they find the youngest layers at the top and the oldest at the bottom. From the evidence of the objects that they find they attempt to date the different layers. This is not always as easy as it seems, as the digging of such things as ditches, pits or postholes cuts through earlier layers and often brings older items to the surface. This is sometimes confusing as older items can be found in younger layers.

In many cases archaeological layers will be destroyed through later human activity. This is particularly the case in ploughed areas. Here only the deeper buried features will survive. In the case of towns the situation can be very different. Imagine somebody building a house. After a few generations it is abandoned and it collapses. The ruins are used as a place to throw rubbish. Leaves blow in and plants grow. Soon only an earthen mound is left. Somebody then comes along and decides to

ABOVE **This display shows how layers build up as time passes. Like detectives, archaeologists use objects and other evidence within the layers to date them and get an idea of the lives of the people at that time.**

build on the same spot. Rather than clearing everything away, after creating a roughly level area they build their house on top of the ruins of the old one… and so the process continues.

This building-up of layers is evident in much of Colchester. A height difference can be seen at several locations around the town walls between the inside and the outside of the town. Sir Isaac's Walk, just inside the walls on the south side of the town, is several metres higher than the adjacent St John's Street, just outside the walls. This is a reflection of the building-up of layers in a densely occupied area of the town. Another good example of this building-up of layers can be seen right outside Colchester Castle. In the

LEFT **A spectacular find in 1996 was an early Roman burial at Stanway. Among the grave goods was a gaming-board, complete with all its glass counters laid out as if a game was in progress.**

1930s the ground level was at the height of the main entrance way. An archaeological excavation then took place to reveal the ground level in the early medieval period at the time when the Castle was built, which is what can be seen today under the entrance bridge. The height difference is 2.25 m (7 ft 6 in). The Roman ground surface is, of course, even lower and is still buried under the ground.

It is the job of the archaeologist to strip away these layers of the past and reveal and record the underlying hidden evidence. Many exciting archaeological finds have been made in Colchester and the surrounding area. These have given us both a high quality and a wide variety of archaeological collections, which are now on display in Colchester Castle Museum. Though much has been found and new exciting discoveries are being made all the time there will always be far more to be revealed, and so the detective work continues.

ABOVE
A reconstruction of the graveside ceremony at another wealthy grave at Stanway.

The Beginning: from Stone Age to Bronze Age

ABOVE **A modern craftsman, John Lord, demonstrates the ancient skill of flint-knapping in the prehistoric gallery at Colchester Castle Museum. This is one of a number of events and activities that take place during the school holidays.**

ABOVE **A polished neolithic flint axe from around 4000 BC, found near Lawford.**

RIGHT **The Dagenham Idol. This wooden figure dates from around 2500 BC. It was found 6 m (20 ft) down in an area of marsh at Dagenham, on the north bank of the Thames.**

LEFT **A bronze cauldron found at Sheepen. It dates to around 1100 BC and is one of the oldest metal cauldrons known from northern Europe.**

The earliest evidence of human beings in this country is dated to around 500,000 years ago. Most of the evidence is in the form of stone tools. The most characteristic tool type of these early times is called a handaxe, which seems to have been used for general-purpose chopping and cutting. Many hundreds have been found in Essex.

During the hundreds of thousands of years of the Palaeolithic or Old Stone Age the climate shifted between periods of intense cold (ice ages or glacials), when ice sheets spread over much of Britain and Western Europe, and warm spells (interglacials), when the ice retreated and the climate was more hospitable, sometimes even warmer than today.

About 10,000 years ago the last ice age ended. As the ice sheets retreated, so the sea-level rose, leading to the separation of Britain from the mainland of Europe. The country became covered by dense forests of oak and elm in which deer, elk, wild pigs and many other large animals lived. The prehistoric inhabitants of the area lived by hunting these wild animals and gathering the fruits, nuts,

roots and berries of the forests. These people lived a nomadic lifestyle.

In about 4000 BC these people began to farm, which led to a new, more settled way of life. This is the period known as the Neolithic or New Stone Age. To create space for fields to grow crops or graze livestock the Neolithic farmers had to clear the thick forests and they developed stone axes that were well suited to this task.

The first metal objects were introduced into Britain just before 2000 BC, and this period is known as the Bronze Age. Bronze is an alloy, made by mixing tin and copper. The introduction of ironworking around 700 BC allowed access to a more easily available metal than bronze. Iron quickly displaced it for working tools, though bronze continued to be used for decorative purposes. This period is known as the Iron Age.

Camulodunum

In the late Iron Age the peoples of southern Britain were split into a series of separate tribes or kingdoms. Each kingdom had a monarch or ruler. In Essex the local people were known as the Trinovantes and they were often at war with the neighbouring tribe to the west, the Catuvellauni.

By 25 BC the tribal capital of the Trinovantes had been established in the area of modern Colchester. It was called Camulodunum which translates as 'the Fortress of Camulos'. Camulos was a Celtic god of war. Camulodunum covered an area of 32 square kilometres (12 sq miles). It was protected by a series of massive banks and ditches (dykes). These gave protection from attack, but also demonstrated the great power of the kings. The dyke system can still be seen today, particularly to the west of the town.

The most powerful of the early kings of Britain was Cunobelin, who reigned from about 5 BC to AD 40. He was king of both the Trinovantes and the Catuvellauni. The extent of his power spread even further as is seen through his gold coins, which are found all over south-east Britain. To the Romans he was not a simple tribal leader. He was Rex Britannorum – 'King of the Britons'.

The wealth and status of the native British aristocracy can be seen in their graves. These often contain luxury goods imported from the continent. This was certainly the case at Lexden in Colchester where a burial had been placed in a large wooden chamber, sunk into the ground and covered with a mound. Though the grave goods only survive as broken fragments, their quality shows that this must have been a royal grave. Probably the most fascinating object with the burial was a medallion depicting the Roman Emperor Augustus. This is likely to have been a gift from the Emperor to a neighbouring king.

Two sides of a gold coin of Cunobelin. On one side is a running horse, below which is written CVN (short for Cunobelin), and on the other is an ear of corn with the letters CAM (short for Camulodunum).

CENTRE **A silver medallion from the Lexden tumulus, depicting the Roman Emperor Augustus.**

BELOW **A hoard of broken metal objects dating from the Later Bronze Age, found at Hatfield Broad Oak.**

LEFT **An unusual piece of pottery decorated with a mounted Iron Age warrior, found during an excavation at Kelvedon. Of special note is the spiked hair of the warrior and the fact that he is not carrying a spear but rather something that looks like a shepherd's crook.**

The Roman Invasion

The tombstone of Marcus Favonius Facilis, a centurion of the 20th Legion. Facilis is believed to have been a member of the invading Roman army who died while serving at Colchester in the early years after the conquest.

RIGHT **A bronze object adorned with a circle of running animals, dating from the early years of the Roman occupation. Found at Sheepen, it is thought to be a tool for decorating leatherwork.**

RIGHT **Dressing for action. A young visitor feels the weight of Roman armour.**

The Romans were well aware of the importance of Camulodunum. The Emperors Augustus and Gaius (Caligula) both considered invading Britain but it was only after Cunobelin's death, in about AD 40, that serious plans for conquest were made.

In AD 41 Claudius became Emperor of Rome. His hold on power was weak and he needed to strengthen it. One of the best ways to do this was to gain popularity through military conquest, and Britain was an obvious target.

In April AD 43 a Roman army, led by the general Aulus Plautius, set sail for the shores of Britain. They landed in Kent and, as the capture of Camulodunum was their principal objective, they began to march north.

The Romans fought various battles against the Britons, who were led by Cunobelin's sons Caratacus and Togodumnus. In one battle Togodumnus was killed, and gradually the Britons retreated towards Camulodunum.

As the Roman army approached Camulodunum, Claudius arrived

LEFT **A bronze copy of the head of the Emperor Claudius, found in the River Alde in Suffolk in 1907. It may have originally come from the Temple of Claudius in Colchester.**

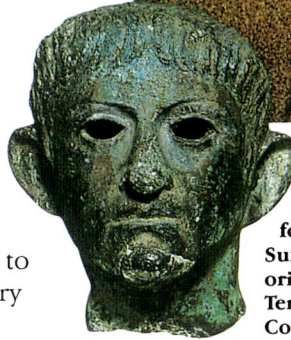

from Italy to take personal charge of the attack on this British stronghold. The Romans quickly captured the Iron Age capital. The Britons, already demoralised, were no match for the organised Roman army, whose attack may have been made even more terrifying by the use of elephants, an animal the Britons would never have seen before.

Though the Britons were not yet totally defeated, many now recognised the Romans as victorious, and a number of British tribal kings surrendered to Claudius while he was at Camulodunum.

It was important for the Romans to keep control of the native capital so they built a fortress on the hilltop, where Colchester's modern town centre now stands. By about AD 49 the fortress was replaced by a town. This became the first capital of the new Roman province.

RIGHT **Scorched Samian ware pottery from a Roman shop in Colchester that was burnt down during the Boudican revolt.**

Boudica's Revenge

ABOVE **Queen Boudica and her army. This is an illustration from *The Revenge*, an audio-visual display that explains the reason behind the sacking of Colchester by Boudica in AD 60.**

ABOVE RIGHT **The missing face of Longinus, a spectacular find made in 1996. The face fits perfectly back onto the tombstone (right) found in 1928.**

At Colchester, in the early years after the Roman invasion, life for many of the Britons was harsh. Many had their homes and land stolen by the new Roman settlers.

Some were forced into slavery and were made to build a grand temple dedicated to the Roman Emperor Claudius.

In AD 60 a revolt against the Romans broke out. It was led by Boudica (popularly known as Boadicea), who was queen of

the Iceni, a tribe that lived in the area of modern Norfolk and north Suffolk. There were many reasons for the revolt, but the spark that started it was an assault on Boudica and her two daughters by Roman soldiers and the seizure of royal property after the death of her husband, Prasutagus.

Boudica led her army south to attack Colchester, the capital of Roman Britain. In the town was the grand Temple of Claudius, which was a symbol to the Britons of their oppression by the Romans, 'the citadel of an eternal tyranny' as described by the Roman historian Tacitus.

The main body of the Roman army was too far away to provide help, and the town had no real defences. Confronted with Boudica's army the

townspeople fell back to the area of the Temple. After a two-day siege the last defences were broken and everyone inside was killed.

Leaving Colchester a smouldering ruin, Boudica led her army to destroy the Roman settlements at London and St Albans before being finally defeated. Boudica escaped but later committed suicide and was buried in a secret location by her people.

RIGHT **Roman soldier's helmet reconstructed from fragments found in a pit at Sheepen. It dates to around the period of the Boudican revolt as can be seen from the burnt edging.**

Tombstone of a Roman auxiliary cavalryman called Longinus Sdapeze. Like the Roman centurion, he died while based in Colchester and would have served with the invading Roman army. The tombstone was found in 1928 at Lexden Road, in Colchester. His face was found in 1996 (left).

LEFT **Slave for sale. Children find out what it was like to wear a Roman slave chain.**

9

Roman Life

ABOVE **A few of the many Roman glass vessels found in Colchester. The museum's collection of Roman glass is one of the finest in Britain.**

ABOVE **Try on a toga! The toga is more than 5 m (almost 6 yds) in length, and you need help from someone else to put it on.**

ABOVE
An elaborate Roman brooch, delicately decorated with coloured enamels, found in Colchester.

After the Boudican revolt Colchester was rebuilt on top of the burnt ruins. This time, though, the precaution was taken to surround the town with strong walls, which can still be seen today. It developed into a large and wealthy town and, even though it lost its role as the capital of the province, it remained one of the most important towns in Roman Britain. The Temple of Claudius was rebuilt and was the most important of many temples within the town and in the surrounding area. The town boasted two theatres, one in the area of modern-day Maidenburgh Street and the other on the outskirts at Gosbecks. It was the hub of a network of roads leading out into the surrounding countryside and on to other Roman settlements and towns.

ABOVE **A decorative roof-fitting – an antefix – depicting the head of Medusa, a Greek mythical figure, that once adorned a house in Roman Colchester.**

LEFT **This statue of the Roman god Mercury was found at Gosbecks, just to the south-west of the town. It ranks as one of the finest Roman bronze sculptures so far found in Britain.**

The builders of Roman Colchester faced a major problem: the lack of good quality, local building stone. They overcame this mainly by using local clay to make bricks and tiles. They also used the poor local stone, bonded with mortar, for the foundations of their major buildings, as can be seen in the surviving parts of the Temple of Claudius which form the foundations of the Castle.

Inside the walls the town developed on a grid pattern, with its main street running roughly along the line of the modern High Street. The residents had an efficient drainage and water supply system. A surviving example of one of the large barrel-vaulted drains can be seen on the edge of the Castle Park, just to the north-west of the Castle.

RIGHT **The Colchester Vase, found in 1848, is one of the finest examples of ceramic art from Roman Britain. It depicts four gladiators and a hunting scene.**

LEFT **Get in touch with the past by handling Roman pots.**

ABOVE **Specially designed activities, tailored to the National Curriculum, bring history alive for school children.**

The wealthier houses in the town were elaborate. They would have had features such as underfloor heating (hypocaust systems) and they were often richly decorated with frescoes (painted plaster), which covered the walls, and with mosaics on the floors. Roman Colchester has in fact produced one of the largest concentrations of mosaics known from Roman Britain. It is believed that in Colchester there was a specialist workshop, or school, devoted to the design and production of mosaics.

Roman Colchester was also a centre for industry. In particular, a large pottery industry developed around the town. This produced everything from coarse, everyday-pots for

cooking and storage to fine vessels only to be used on special occasions. Some of the finest wares ever produced in Roman Britain were made in Colchester. Colchester is the only place in Britain that is definitely known to have produced Samian ware, one of the most distinctive types of Roman fine pottery.

Much of the industry was devoted to supplying the needs of the town but it also produced a lot of material for external trade. The trade was, of course, not one way, goods would have been constantly flowing in from other parts of Britain or the continent, along the road network or along the rivers. The luxury goods, which were imported by the Romans, have since been discovered by archaeologists in excavations in Colchester. These are a further reflection of the town's wealth and status.

BELOW **The Middleborough Mosaic. This fine mosaic floor, found in 1979, once adorned a wealthy Roman house that lay just outside the town walls to the north.**

Death and Burial in Roman Colchester

ABOVE **To learn more about the Christian lady from the Butt Road cemetery (referred to as Camilla) it was decided to flesh out the bare bones. Her skull was sent a leading expert in this kind of work, Richard Neave, who reconstructed her face. The result is that for the first time we can gaze on the face one of Colchester's Roman citizens.**

Roman law decreed that the dead should be buried in cemeteries outside the boundaries of a settlement. In the case of Colchester this meant outside the town walls. Given the size and wealth of Colchester, these cemeteries were extensive.

Many of the roads leading out of Colchester, particularly those to London, would have been lined with burials, which were often marked by elaborate tombstones. The main reason that Colchester has such a fine and large collection of Roman pots is due to the Roman tradition of placing objects in graves, with most burials being accompanied by at least one pottery or glass vessel.

One of the largest of the Roman cemetery areas investigated by archaeologists is at Butt Road, to the south-west of the town. In around AD 330 a rectangular building with a semicircular end (known as an apse) was constructed within the cemetery. Based on its east-west orientation, its plan and the evidence found within, this building is believed to have been a church.

The layout of the cemetery was reoriented around the church. One of these Christian graves consisted of a buried timber chamber containing

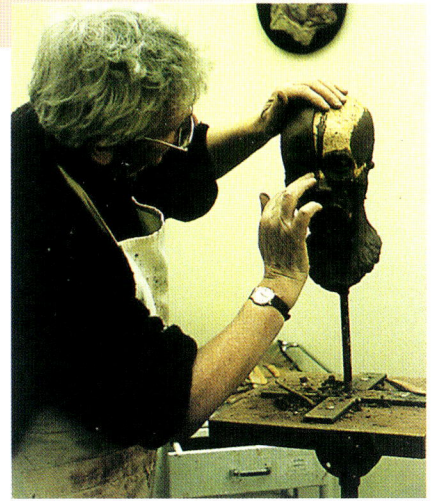

ABOVE **Richard Neave, of the School of Biological Sciences at the University of Manchester, carries out his work of reconstructing Camilla, a face from the past.**

BELOW **The Colchester Sphinx. This fine sculpture, found in 1821, formed part of an elaborate Roman tomb that once stood outside the town walls to the west.**

two bodies in wooden coffins. These were of a man and woman in their forties, and it is believed that they were husband and wife. From the relatively elaborate nature of the burial it is clear that they were wealthy. From their bones we know that the woman was about 1.6 m (5 ft 3 in) tall and that the man had suffered a serious head injury, from which he had recovered.

ABOVE **A Roman burial (AD 125–200), found outside the town walls to the south. The cremated body was placed within the pot, which has been decorated with a face.**

RIGHT **Pottery figures – some of the group of objects found in a Roman grave, known as 'The Child's Grave' (AD 50–60).**

ABOVE **An illustration reconstructing the earliest-known Christian church in Britain, at Butt Road, which was built around AD 330.**

The Saxon and Norman Town

By the start of the fifth century, Roman society in Britain was crumbling, and new Saxon settlers were starting to arrive in Essex from across the North Sea. The Saxons were not used to living in towns and so, after the abandonment of Britain by the Romans in AD 410, Colchester rapidly declined and the buildings fell into ruin. However, the memory of Colchester as a place of ancient importance remained.

Colchester began to grow again in importance in the late Saxon period. The Danes, who had been occupying eastern England, were expelled from the town by Edward the Elder in 917, and he refortified it as a royal centre. King Athelstan in 931 and King Edmund in 940 held councils there. A coin mint was in operation by 991 and also a market. However, much of the area inside the Roman walls remained open land.

After the Norman Conquest in 1066 Colchester saw dramatic growth. At the time of the 'Domesday' survey in 1086 it was ranked fifth equal in England in terms of tax and had a population of about 2,500. In about 1076, because of Colchester's strategic importance on the route from East Anglia to London, William the Conqueror ordered his Steward, Eudo de Rie, to build a castle in stone – the keep of which is the largest ever constructed by the Normans. The Benedictine Abbey of St John was founded in 1095, again by Eudo de Rie, and St Botolph's Priory was refounded in about 1100 as the first Augustinian abbey in Britain.

These buildings were imposing symbols of the feudal society established by the Normans. Everyone owed allegiance in the form of labour, money and services to their immediate lord, who in return had a duty to provide protection and justice. It was a strict hierarchy with the leading churchmen and nobles at the top and the king above them all.

LEFT **A silvered bronze belt-end with an interlaced animal, dating from the tenth century, found in the Castle Park.**

LEFT BELOW **Female carving, dating from the twelfth century, known as a 'sheila-na-gig', from Easthorpe church.**

ABOVE **Illumination of St Michael slaying the dragon from the Colchester Anti-phonary (a choir book). This manuscript was written and illuminated for a Franciscan friary in Italy about 1260.**

LEFT *Earthly Honour*, **a wall-hanging by artist Lisa Wharton. It is used with school groups to demonstrate the feudal relationship between the king and his people in Norman England.**

13

Gallery Guide to Colchester Castle Museum

Roof

The museum's displays have been divided into different historical periods. These are colour-coded on this gallery tour illustration. They are also used throughout this guide at the top outside corner of each double-page spread from page 4 to 19. A key to the colour-coding can be found below.

The Roman vaults, Great Stairs, roof and chapel can only be seen by taking a Blue Badge Guided Tour. These are available five times a day.

Also listed are the outstanding items in the Colchester collection of artefacts. This will help you find them if you have limited time for your visit to the Castle Museum.

Chapel

Crypt

Stairs down

Great Stairs

Lecture Theatre Events Room

Great Stairs

Lift

Great Stairs

9

8

7

7

Toilets

Temporary Exhibition Area

Refreshment Area

First Floor

Stairs

COLOUR KEY TO GALLERIES

- What is Archaeology?
- Stone Age and Bronze Age
- Iron Age
- Roman Invasion
- Boudican Revolt
- Roman Life
- Medieval and Tudor
- Stuart and Civil War
- The Prisons
- Temporary Exhibitions
- Toilets, refreshment area and museum shop

Outstanding Items in Colchester's Collection

1. Mercury (see page 10)
2. Sphinx (see page 12)
3. Colchester Vase (see page 11)
4. Dagenham Idol (see page 6)
5. Sheepen Cauldron (see page 6)
6. Lexden Medallion (see page 7)
7. Facilis and Longinus Tombstones (see pages 8 & 9)
8. Middleborough Mosaic (see page 11)
9. Camilla – the Roman Lady (see page 12)
10. Henry V's Royal Charter of 1413 (see page 16)

Prisons

Stairs

Museum Shop

Well House

Parnell Vault

Great Stairs

Reception Desk

Stairs

Ground Floor

Foundations

Roman Vaults

Illustration by Peter Froste

Medieval and Tudor Colchester

ABOVE **A wall-painting of a young woman, dating from about 1370. The painting came from Park Farm, St Osyth, and was probably associated with St Osyth's Priory.**

RIGHT **Pottery roof finial in the form of a king, dating from the late thirteenth to early fourteenth century, found at Queen Street.**

BELOW **Hats were worn throughout the medieval period. Today, visitors can try on a variety of hats and find out who would have worn them.**

In 1189 the town received its first Royal Charter from Richard I. This gave the wealthier citizens various rights to manage local affairs, including markets, the Colne fisheries and judicial arrangements. These privileges were confirmed and extended by successive charters; that of King Edward III in 1362 gave the town's burgesses (officials) the right to hunt fox, hare and polecat – an unusual and unique privilege.

Colchester remained the largest and in many respects the principal town in Essex throughout the Middle Ages. Local industry included pottery kilns at Middleborough, just outside the North Gate, and leather-working, which reached its peak in the early fourteenth century. The town also had a port, which moved to its present site at the Hythe from Old Heath in about the eleventh century. However, because of the shallowness of the River Colne it never developed into a major port and consequently much of Colchester's trade was carried out through London.

The later medieval wealth of Colchester was founded on the cloth trade. In the fourteenth and fifteenth centuries the town gained a reputation all over Europe for the manufacture of russet and, later, fine grey cloths. The principal destinations were Prussia and Gascony in south-west France. Timber, wine and

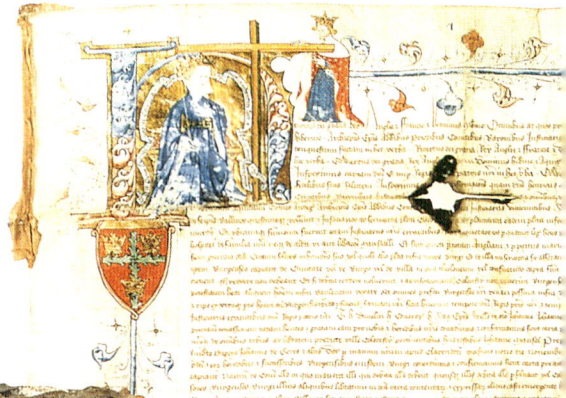

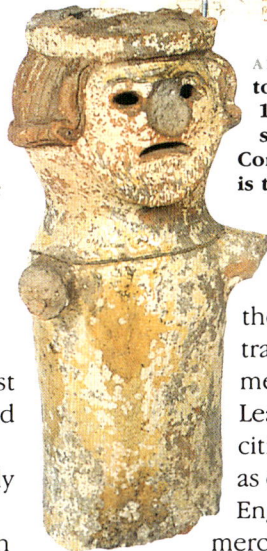

ABOVE **The Royal Charter granted to Colchester by King Henry V in 1413. It shows the town's patron saint, Helena, with her son Constantine the Great. Below her is the earliest-known representation of the Borough's coat of arms.**

fine pottery were among the goods brought back. The trade attracted a colony of merchants from the Hanseatic League, an alliance of German cities, who selected Colchester as one of their principal English depots. Italian merchants based in London were also keen buyers.

Growing wealth was reflected in the appearance of the town. Buildings increased in size while window-glass replaced wooden shutters. Inside, wattle and daub walls were covered in painted plaster or wood

RIGHT **This Flemish carved wooden bench-end shows St Dunstan. Dating from the late fifteenth century, it is reputed to have been taken from St Botolph's Priory during the Siege of Colchester in 1648.**

ABOVE **Feel the quality! A roll of (modern) Colchester bay cloth draws attention to the importance of the cloth trade to the town in the past.**

LEFT **Medieval pottery from Colchester in a reconstruction of a medieval kitchen, complete with rat!**

ABOVE **Table mats painted with fruit, flowers and verses – late sixteenth century.**

LEFT **A saddle, dating from the sixteenth century, which was reputedly used by Queen Elizabeth I when she visited Sir Thomas Smith at Hill Hall near Theydon Mount, Essex.**

BELOW **Sir Thomas Lucas (1531–1611) by Robert Peake, about 1595. Lucas owned St John's Abbey and served as Sheriff of Essex and MP and Recorder for Colchester.**

panelling, floors were tiled and fireplaces with chimneys became a popular addition.

By the sixteenth century the cloth trade was in decline. However, from 1565 the town authorities welcomed large groups of skilled Dutch weavers who had fled from Spanish religious persecution in their homeland. The Dutch were granted special privileges and established Colchester as the main centre for the manufacture of the 'new draperies', which were light wool cloths known as bays and says.

At each stage of bay-making the cloth had to be inspected at the Dutch Bay Hall, on the High Street, to ensure that it was of high enough quality. Weavers presenting sub-standard cloth were fined and had their cloth rejected.

This quality control meant that Colchester bays and says were accepted in Europe and the New World purely on inspection of the seals. Tudor Colchester was home to a number of prominent people. Thomas, Lord Audley, (1488–1544) of Berechurch Hall rose from Town Clerk of Colchester to Lord Chancellor of England under King Henry VIII. Sir Thomas Lucas (1531–1611), who owned St John's Abbey, entertained Queen Elizabeth I on her tour of Essex and Suffolk in 1579. William Gilberd (1544–1603), who was Physician and a trusted advisor to Queen Elizabeth I, lived at Tymperleys in Trinity Street. He was a pioneering scientist, proving that the Earth is a magnet, and being the first to research electricity.

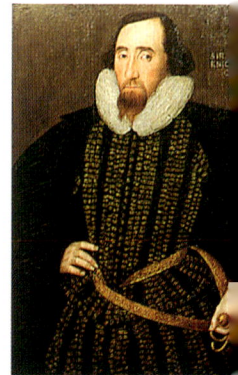

The Stuarts and the Siege of Colchester

A sixteenth-century carved corner-post in the form of the Green Man. It is from a building that stood at the junction of High Street and West Stockwell Street, on the site of the present Town Hall. The Green Man is an ancient symbol of growth and fertility.

The seventeenth century was a time of wildly varying fortunes for Colchester. The population at first expanded rapidly on the success of the cloth trade, reaching about 11,000 in 1620. Most of the town's overseas trade was with Rotterdam, but Colchester ships voyaged the length of the English east coast exchanging cloth and agricultural produce such as cheese, butter, grain and wood for goods such as coal and salt from Newcastle and wool, oil and soap from London.

An insight into the more exotic goods that were arriving in Colchester was unearthed by archaeologists at Lion Walk in 1973. They found two pits full of pots that had once belonged to the Colchester apothecary Robert Buxton (1577–1665). The pots were probably thrown away when Buxton's shop, called The Old Twisted Posts and Pots, was cleared out after he had retired in the 1650s. Apothecaries were the equivalent of today's High Street chemists. However, they also invented and made their own medicines from natural ingredients. Their shops were full of strange preserved animals and strong-smelling herbs and spices from around the world.

CENTRE Tin-glazed jar, about 1640, excavated at Lion Walk from the site of Robert Buxton's apothecary shop.

RIGHT A reconstruction of a Parliamentary foot soldier in camp during the Siege of Colchester in 1648.

Robert Buxton served as Mayor of Colchester in 1636 and 1645 at a time of increasing tension in the town. The cloth trade brought huge wealth to bay-makers such as the Tayspill family, but the ordinary weavers were at the mercy of fluctuations in the trade. Whenever the trade slumped, as it did in the 1640s, there was the danger of riots. Religious rivalries also often led to disturbances in this radically Protestant town.

Colchester backed Parliament against King Charles I during the Civil War (1642–51), providing troops, horses and money for the cause. In August 1642 an angry crowd looted Sir John Lucas' house at St John's Abbey and imprisoned him in the Moot Hall on suspicion of gathering

18

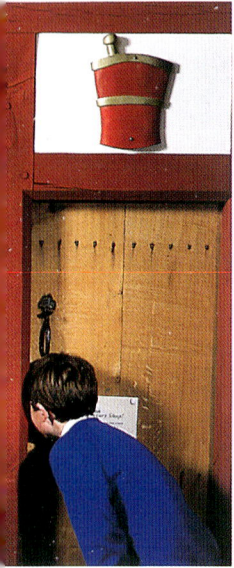

LEFT **A reconstruction of a seventeenth-century apothecary shop, using traditional carpentry skills. The shop contains the contents of Robert Buxton's apothecary, called 'The Old Twisted Posts and Pots', excavated at Lion Walk in 1973.**

Sir George Lisle were held in the Castle in what is now called the Lucas Vault and then executed outside the Castle by firing squad. This spot is now marked by an obelisk.

A further setback to the town occurred less than twenty years later with the return of the Black Death. It had first

CENTRE **Funerary helmet from the tomb of Royalist leader Sir Charles Lucas in St Giles' Church, Colchester.**

BELOW **Shot for a Civil War artillery piece known as a rabonett, found under the floor of a barn near Colchester.**

arms to help the King. By 1648 the Royalists had been defeated, and the war seemed over.

However, a few die-hard Royalists, including Sir Charles Lucas (Sir John Lucas' brother), raised a new force in Kent and marched on London. They were beaten off and moved into Essex, making for Norfolk. On 12 June 1648 they arrived at the gates of Colchester. Under threat, the townspeople agreed to let them in, expecting them to stay for a day. However, the Parliamentarian army, led by Sir Thomas Fairfax, arrived. They failed to storm the town and so settled in for a siege which was to last seventy-six days.

The siege had a devastating effect on Colchester. The town was heavily bombarded, and many buildings, including St Botolph's Priory, were destroyed or damaged. The townspeople were besieged by an army that they largely supported. They slowly starved during one of the coldest and wettest summers known and were reduced to eating dogs, rats and candles. In a final blow at the end of the siege the town was ordered to pay the enormous fine of £12,000 (more than £2m today) for harbouring the enemy. Sir Charles Lucas and his fellow Royalist commander

arrived in Colchester during the winter of 1348. More than 1,000 people died – about a quarter of the town's population. For the next three centuries the plague remained present in the town at a low level. In the summer of 1665 it flared up in a final epidemic that spread from London. About 4,500 people died – half the population of Colchester. This remains the worst epidemic of modern times in England.

The town, though, recovered quickly from both disasters to finish the century largely as it had started. Cloth was the main, but fickle, source of wealth for many, and religious debate was a major driving force in town life and politics.

ABOVE **A plan of the Siege of Colchester, 1648, showing the encircling Parliamentary forts.**

BELOW **A painting of *The Execution of Sir Charles Lucas and Sir George Lisle*, attributed to Benjamin Strutt, about 1800.**

The Construction of Colchester Castle

BELOW **The Temple of Claudius, showing the sand-filled vaults that formed the foundations.**

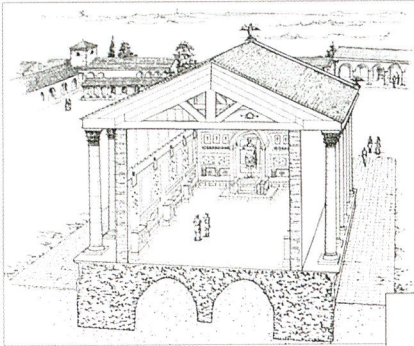

BELOW AND RIGHT **The Normans incorporated the platform of the Temple of Claudius into the foundations of the Castle keep. It is the largest keep ever built and in about 1200 may have resembled the reconstruction below.**

It is not known precisely when construction of the Castle began but building is thought to have been under way by 1076. The Normans were faced with the same problem that the Romans had a thousand years before: a lack of good-quality building stone. The Norman solution was to dig up Roman Colchester to provide most of the raw materials they needed.

This problem over stone also probably had a great deal to do with the siting of the Castle. Strategically, it would have better on the higher ground butting onto the town wall at the west end of the town. Instead, the site of the ruined Temple of Claudius was chosen. The traditional use of this area may have played its part, but the presence of the great stone base of the Temple must have been decisive as it gave the Norman builders a head start in constructing a castle.

The Castle, or rather the keep (the central tower element of a castle), was the largest ever built by the Normans, measuring 46.18 by 33.5 m (151 by 110 ft).

In plan the Castle has two major elements, a square and a rectangular block, with a semicircular end on the south side. This ground-plan is shared by only one other castle in the country, the White Tower (the Tower of London), which was built slightly later than that of Colchester. It is believed that Gundulph, Bishop of Rochester, was responsible for the design of the Tower of London and it seems highly probable that he was also involved at Colchester.

The construction of the Castle keep can be divided into two main phases. The first-phase keep was only one storey high as is shown by the traces of battlements which can still be seen clearly on some areas of the outer walls. This may have been the original design or a temporary solution to deal with a period of emergency. Whatever the reason, a second phase of construction saw the walls raised higher, though how high is the subject of major debate.

Surrounding the keep was a large bank-and-ditch, of which only the north and east sections survive substantially intact. Within this area, called the bailey, would have been many other buildings such as stables, storehouses and work-shops. On the north side a further bank-and-ditch system, creating a lower bailey, extended down to the town walls.

The Castle was a royal fortress throughout the Middle Ages and was only entrusted to loyal supporters of the king. It only saw serious action once, in 1216, when King John had to retake it from a French occupying force. The French had been sent by King Philip of France to assist the English barons in their rebellion against John, which had led to the signing of the Magna Carta the previous year.

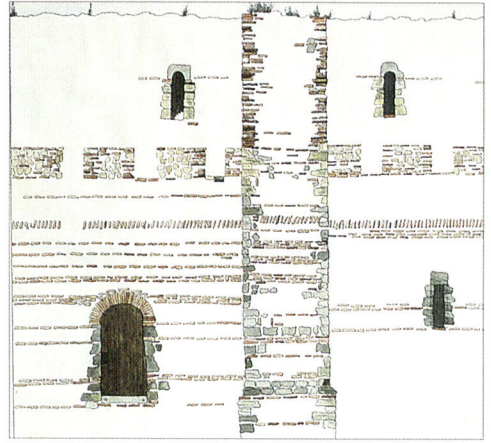

ABOVE **This sketch of the Castle walls by K.C. Scarff clearly shows the battlements of the first-phase castle.**

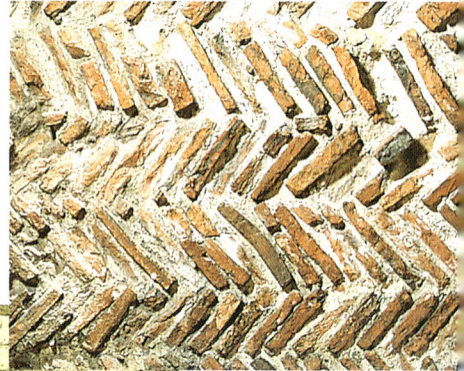

ABOVE **Reused Roman tiles laid in a herringbone pattern in the surviving internal dividing wall.**

LEFT **Close-up of the Norman arch over the entrance doorway. It is partly built of Caen stone brought from Normandy.**

Interior Features of Colchester Castle

RIGHT **A chimney on the first floor. The Y-shaped flue design is a very rare architectural feature.**

ABOVE **A window on the Great Stairs, piercing the 3.5 m (11 ft) bulk of the Castle walls.**

RIGHT **The entrance to the Great Stairs – the largest-diameter winding staircase in Britain.**

BELOW **Two examples of graffiti to be seen on the Great Stairs: a Norman soldier and knight, and a flower design that was a good luck symbol in the sixteenth century.**

RIGHT **One of the medieval toilets, known as a garderobe, on the first floor.**

Only a limited amount is known about the interior layout of the Castle due to its ruinous state. Understanding of the use of some areas is also greatly affected by doubts over the original height of the Castle. This is particularly true for the location of a chapel, which is known to have existed from documentary evidence. In the eighteenth century, the massive barrel-vaulted room at the south-east corner of the first floor was referred to as 'the chapel'.

In the later nineteenth century, comparison with the White Tower (the Tower of London), led to the theory that Colchester Castle originally extended up a further two storeys, making it four storeys in all. Today, the standard interpretation is that the Castle was built with only three storeys and that the original design may have been modified before completion. Both these theories place the chapel at the present roof level in the area above 'Gray's chapel' which became known as the crypt. The discovery of foundations on the roof in 1908 seemed to support this view. In 1988 these structures were further investigated and a modern roof was placed over them.

However, new evidence and re-thinking of the arguments suggests that the Castle was always roughly at

the height it is today, though with the main walls slightly higher and with towers at the four corners. This could place the chapel back where Charles Gray considered it to be.

Though there is doubt over the use of certain areas, many important internal features do survive. Of special note is the main staircase, the Great Stairs, on the west side of the entrance way, which at 4.8 m (16 ft) is the largest-diameter newel (winding) staircase in Britain.

Some particularly interesting features can be found on the first floor. There are four fireplaces, two each in the east and west walls, which are early examples of their kind, having y-shaped chimneys that discharge, not on the roof, but through holes in the walls. There are also examples of the basic but effective medieval toilets, known as garderobes. These consist of stone seats below which is a chute opening out onto the Castle walls.

Later History of the Castle

Much of the Castle was in a ruinous state by the sixteenth century. There were various attempts to demolish it. The most determined was by John Wheeley, a local ironmonger, who acquired the Castle in 1683. It was probably Wheeley who first broke through into the Roman vaults beneath the Castle.

In 1727 the Castle was given as a wedding present to Charles Gray, a

study, was added to the north-east tower. Gray mistakenly believed that the Castle was completely Roman and therefore gave the building its Italian-style roof of red tile.

On Gray's death in 1782 the Castle passed to the Round family. In 1920 the Castle came into public ownership, being sold to the Borough by Captain E.J. Round as a war memorial. By the early 1930s, concern at the condition of the vaults, weakened by exposure to the elements, led to the decision to roof over the open courtyard. At the same time a

ABOVE **Charles Gray (1696–1782), antiquarian and MP for Colchester, showing visitors his restoration of the Castle.**

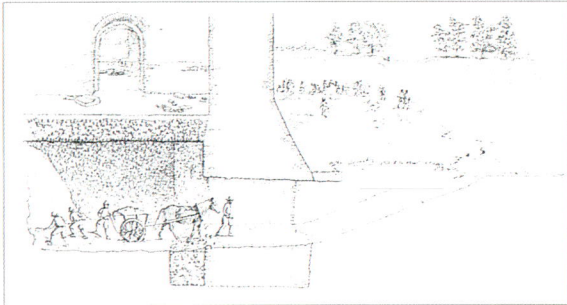

local lawyer and antiquarian who was MP for Colchester from 1747. He lived in Hollytrees, the Georgian mansion nearby, and set about the 'restoration' of the romantic ruin in his back garden. Using the services of a local architect, James Deane, he made some major alterations. The southern end was made habitable again. Large windows for a library were inserted in the south front and also in the apse. The domed top or cupola was placed on the south-west tower, and the small room, which he used as a

new footbridge was built over the recently excavated outer works.

During the Second World War the vaults were used as an air-raid shelter. A bomb fell just to the north but fortunately did not explode. A major programme of conservation and stabilisation of the outside walls of the Castle was begun in 1983 and completed in 1992.

LEFT **One of the large windows inserted into the south front of the Castle by Charles Gray in the eighteenth century.**

LEFT **John Wheeley's attempts to demolish the Castle with gunpowder in the 1690s broke open the Roman foundations and revealed the sand used in its construction. Wheeley started to remove the sand as well as the rubble for the building trade, but he went bankrupt, so saving the Castle from complete destruction.**

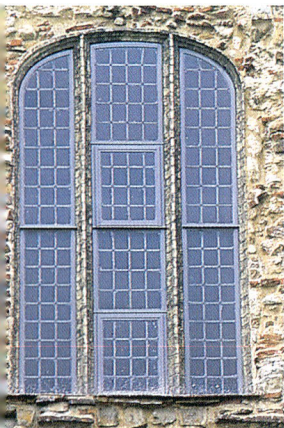

BELOW **An air-raid shelter sign. The Roman vaults were used as a shelter during the Second World War.**

The Castle Prisons

ABOVE **The entrance to the prison cells in the south-east corner of the Castle. They were built in 1727.**

RIGHT **Poignant graffiti: a prisoner's name, 'P. Ley Dec 4 1788', carved into the walls of one of the cells**

RIGHT **The Colchester Martyrs, Margaret Thurston and Agnes Bongeor, burnt at Colchester for their Protestant faith by order of Queen Mary on 17 September 1557.**

The earliest record of the use of Colchester Castle as a gaol is in 1226. People of all kinds, and for all kinds of reason, were imprisoned in the Castle. There were those accused of crimes, including theft, murder, treason, piracy and sedition. Others were held for heretical religious beliefs and for witchcraft. Many hundreds, if not thousands, of prisoners of war were also locked up there at various times.

A large stone-lined pit, preserved under the floor in the area known as the Lucas Vault, may have served as a place to keep a few prisoners in the early years of the Castle. Prison cells, dating from 1727 – complete with massive oak doors and iron-barred windows – survive in the south-east corner of the Castle, but over the years many parts of the Castle were used as accommodation for prisoners and gaolers alike despite its ruinous state at times.

The most celebrated prisoner was Sir Thomas Malory (c. 1410–71), who is believed to be the author of one of the most important pieces of literature about King Arthur and

Camelot, the *Morte d'Arthur*. Malory, from Newbold Revel in Warwickshire, was caught up in the turmoil of the Wars of the Roses. From 1450 onwards, accused of a variety of crimes, including theft, murder, rape and extortion, he spent a great deal of time in prison, including a brief period in October 1454 at the Castle, from which he made a dramatic escape.

From the fourteenth century onwards Colchester was a centre for radical religious believers who challenged the views of the established Church. In 1429 William Chieveling, a tailor, was convicted of being a Lollard – someone who denied the authority of the Pope and Catholic priests. He was burnt at the stake as a heretic in front of the Castle. Chieveling was the first of the 'Colchester Martyrs', all of whom are recorded on a memorial in the Town Hall.

Colchester was quick to embrace Protestantism at the Reformation and became a focal point of opposition to

The Burning of Margaret Thurston & Agnes Bongeor at Colchester.

Queen Mary's Catholic government. The town was described as 'a harbourer of heretics and ever was'. Between 1555 and 1558, twenty-three people were burnt in the town; only London and Canterbury witnessed more burnings.

The last of the martyrs was a young Quaker, James Parnell. In 1655, aged eighteen, he arrived in Essex and preached to large crowds. He was arrested and, when he refused to pay a fine, was imprisoned in the Castle, under the control of a vindictive gaoler, Nicholas Roberts. Roberts and his wife charged Parnell fourpence a night – usual practice at the time – and inter-cepted any food that friends tried to send him. He was imprisoned at first in a cell above the entrance corridor, which was reached by a ladder and a rope. Because of illness, he was moved to the ground-floor cell directly below without heat or light. Here he died on 4 May 1656 and is now remembered on a memorial tablet. The initial verdict on his death was suicide because, too ill, he had 'refused' to eat.

One of the most notorious episodes in the Castle's history was when it was used by Matthew Hopkins, the self-styled 'Witch-Finder General', who operated in East Anglia between 1645 and 1647. There was an increasing fear of witchcraft through the sixteenth and seventeenth centuries and, in the disturbed times of the Civil War, Hopkins found many who were willing to blame their misfortunes on the work of a witch. Hopkins' methods of interrogation involved denying the, almost invariably female, suspect sleep and pricking them with a needle to try and find their 'witch's mark' where they felt no pain. All the while he would be encouraging them to confess and to implicate others. In 1645 in Colchester Castle he made fifteen-year-old Rebecca West from Lawford turn King's evidence against her mother Anne, who was then hanged for bewitching a man to death.

Although the Castle ceased to be the county gaol in 1668, it continued to be used as a prison, even during the time of Charles Gray, who let space at the eastern end for this purpose in 1734. John Howard, the prison reformer, visited Colchester Castle on four occasions and recorded the appalling conditions he found. Just prior to one of his visits, in October 1775, even the head gaoler had succumbed to the insanitary condi-tions, having died of typhus. Despite Howard's protests there is little evidence of any attempt to im-prove matters. The gaol was finally closed in 1835.

ABOVE **Matthew Hopkins, the Witch-Finder General. This print is from his book *The Discovery of Witches*, published in 1647.**

LEFT **Colchester's stocks. They were last used on 4 November 1858, when Anne Balls, aged eighty, was sentenced to six hours on the Town Hall steps for being unable to pay a fine for drunkenness.**

BELOW **The vault, near the Castle's main entrance, in which the Quaker James Parnell died for his faith in 1656.**

Colchester's Museums Services

RIGHT **A Blue Badge Guide points out a feature of the Castle's construction during a tour of the Roman vaults.**

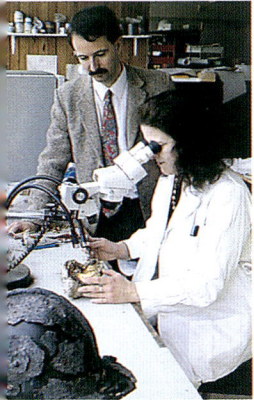

ABOVE **The museum's collections receive detailed attention in the conservation laboratory.**

RIGHT **Who knows the answer? The museum's education service has been recognised nationally as a centre of excellence.**

Blue Badge Guided Tours of the Castle

There are guided tours of the Castle, during museum opening hours, which visit areas not normally open to the public. These include the Roman vaults, the Great Stairs and the rooftop. The Castle roof is an excellent vantage point for views over the town and surrounding countryside. The tours are led by qualified Blue Badge Guides who provide a wealth of interesting details about the Castle and its history. Tours of the town, also conducted by Blue Badge Guides, can be booked at the Visitor Information Centre just opposite the War Memorial entrance to the Castle Park. *Visitor Information Centre, 1 Queen Street, Colchester CO1 1PG. Tel. 01206 282920.*

Colchester Museums' Education Service

The Museum Education Service supports schools by offering a comprehensive set of 'packages' tailored to the National Curriculum. Specialist teacher training helps to extend classroom learning and provide school activities which generate interest and enthusiasm. It aims to encourage other members of the family to visit and to foster a love

for life-long learning. Colchester Museums has a professional team of educators, curators, conservators and interpreters dedicated to explaining the natural and human history of the Colchester area.

Recognised nationally as a centre of excellence for staff development and training, Colchester Museums can offer: Roman and Norman story tours, teacher-training services, professionally produced resource material, a natural history education programme and an outreach service with loan boxes with contents covering the Roman, medieval and Victorian eras.

Identification and Enquiry Service

The museum service operates an identification and enquiry service. Objects to be identified should be brought in person to the Castle Museum. Enquiries are welcomed about the museum collections, the natural and human history of Colchester and advice on conservation of objects. Researchers who wish to visit are requested to make an appointment.

Friends of Colchester Museums

The Friends support Colchester Museums by encouraging people to visit, helping at special events, holding a regular lecture programme and purchasing objects for the museum collections. Friends receive free admission to the Castle Museum, regular newsletters and invitations to special preview evenings. Membership application forms are available at the Castle Museum.

Colchester's Other Museums

Natural History Museum

Hear a mammoth roar, see a pre-historic shark's tooth, touch a fox, see moles underground, see a rabbit and a badger in their burrows and much more at the Natural History Museum. Dare you put your hands in the feely box? A visit to the Natural History Museum tells the story of the animals and plants which have lived in and around Colchester from the Ice Age right up to the present day. The Natural History Museum can be found in All Saints' Church in the High Street.

ABOVE **All Saints' Church – now the home of the Natural History Museum with its emphasis on hands-on experience.**

Hollytrees Museum

Find out what your grandparents and their parents might have played with when they were children. Toys, costume and home furnishings are displayed in Hollytrees, an elegant Georgian townhouse built in 1718 and situated on the edge of Castle Park, opposite the Visitor Information Centre.

RIGHT **Toys and costume of a bygone era are on display in the elegant Georgian setting of Hollytrees.**

Tymperleys Clock Museum

Enjoy the architectural splendour of this fifteenth-century timber-framed house, home to a fine collection of seventeenth-, eighteenth- and nineteenth-century clocks which were made in Colchester. Tymperleys Clock Museum can be found in Trinity Street.

ABOVE **Just one of a collection of exquisite clocks made in Colchester which can be found in Tymperleys.**

The address for all museum correspondence is:
Colchester Museums
Museum Resource Centre
14 Ryegate Road
Colchester CO1 1YG.

Telephone:
General enquiries: 01206 282931/2
Castle Museum: 01206 282939
School bookings and events:
01206 282937

Colchester's Historic Sites

The Dyke System

Camulodunum was not a town in the modern sense but was more like a large country estate. Its commercial, industrial and farming settlements were enclosed and protected by an elaborate system of earthworks or dykes, much of which survives today to the west of the town.

ABOVE **Gryme's Dyke – part of the Iron Age bank-and-ditch system that defended the ancient settlement of Camulodunum.**

Gosbecks

Gosbecks, on the south-western edge of the town, is the original site of Cunobelin's royal seat at Camulodunum. After the Roman invasion, Gosbecks was allowed to continue as a flourishing native centre, watched over initially by a Roman fort which could house 500 soldiers. Nearby, the largest of the five known Roman theatres in Britain was built with seating for up to 5,000 people. There was also an impressive Romano-Celtic temple complex. The finest bronze figure from Roman Britain ever found, the Colchester Mercury, was discovered nearby and is on display in the Castle Museum. Gosbecks is now being preserved as an Archaeological Park, and its various historic features are explained on site.

The Town Walls

The Romans quickly rebuilt the town after its destruction by Boudica in AD 60. The new town was enclosed by a substantial defensive wall. Some two thirds of these defences still stand, making Colchester's town walls the oldest in Britain. Of particular importance is the **Balkerne Gate** (*above*), the original main entrance to the town, which probably began as a triumphal arch celebrating the conquest by Claudius.

Roman Church

Many cemeteries have been discovered in the south and west of the town. These have produced elaborate grave goods which can be seen in the Castle Museum today. On the edge of the main cemetery, at Butt Road, is the site of the earliest-known Christian church in Britain, dating from the fourth century. Its foundations are now displayed beside the police station on Southway.

Roman Theatre

A walk through the historic Dutch Quarter, just off the High Street, will take you through some of Colchester's most picturesque streets. Here, part of the remains of a Roman theatre have been left uncovered under 74 Maidenburgh Street. The outline of the theatre has

Museum History

ABOVE **Miss Smith, the 'Keeper of the Castle', with a party of visitors in about 1850. Miss Smith was born in the Castle and lived all her life there.**

The museum collections were started by the Council in 1846 in a room at the Town Hall. In 1855 the owner of the Castle, Charles Gray Round, allowed part of it to be used as the town museum, though it would be another five years before it was opened to the public (on 27 September 1860). At the beginning the collection occupied just the room known as the crypt on the first floor, which had previously been leased to the local militia as an armoury. Over time it grew and came to fill the whole Castle.

Important collections of archaeological material were acquired early in the history of the museum. Of particular importance was the 'Acton Collection', obtained in 1860 and consisting mainly of material collected twenty years earlier by William Wire, a pioneer of the archaeology of Colchester. In 1892 the extensive 'Jarmin Collection' of Roman material from Colchester was

BELOW **A selection of early guides to the museum.**

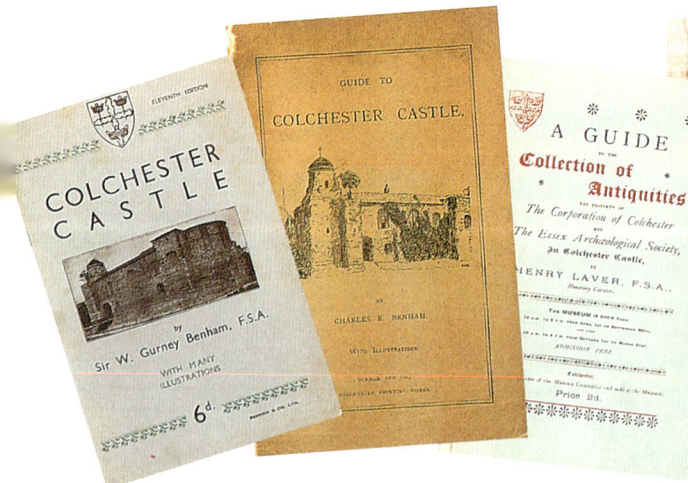

purchased and in 1893 the museum acquired George Joslin's collection from the Colchester Roman Grave Groups. The 'Joslin Collection' is probably the finest private collection of Roman material ever gathered from one locality in Britain. It includes more than one thousand vessels and urns of various kinds as well as one of the most famous objects from Roman Britain, the tombstone of Marcus Favonius Facilis, a centurion of the 20th Legion.

So by the end of the nineteenth century Colchester Castle contained what was probably the finest and most extensive collection of British Roman material existing at the time.

In 1920 the Castle itself was bought by the Borough with money donated by Viscount Cowdray, who had formerly been MP for Colchester. In the early 1930s the open courtyard was roofed over, which created substantial new space to house the growing museum collection. The enlarged museum, entered across a new footbridge over the recently

BELOW **Below Mr A.G. Wright (left), Curator (1902–26), and Alderman Henry Laver, Honorary Curator (1892–1917), who was one of the museum's greatest benefactors.**

CW01429178